# DOVES

LACHLAN MACKINNON

# Doves

for Susan

with my best wishes

Lachlan

ff

FABER & FABER

First published in 2017
by Faber & Faber Ltd
Bloomsbury House
74–77 Great Russell Street
London WC1B 3DA

Typeset by Hamish Ironside
Printed in England by Martins the Printers, Berwick-upon-Tweed

A CIP record for this book is available from the British Library

ISBN 978-0-571-33331-8

2 4 6 8 10 9 7 5 3 1

*I would like to sleep like a child*
*in the hay of an antique summer.*

*I would have liked to live*
*in times I could be proud of.*

# Acknowledgements

Several of these poems have previously appeared in *Dark Horse*, *Guardian* and *Spectator*. 'Lines Written on the Retirement of Mr Peter Conrad' appeared in *Where We Fell to Earth: Writing for Peter Conrad*, eds Michael Dobson and James Woodall (privately published, 2011). '1988' appeared in *Jubilee Lines*, ed. Carol Ann Duffy (Faber & Faber, 2012); 'Christmas Eve' in *Twelve Poems of Christmas* vol. 7, ed. Carol Ann Duffy (Candlestick Press, 2015); 'Joseph Brodsky, 1940–1996' in *From Those Who Remember Me*, ed. Valentina Polukhina (Tomsk, 2015); and 'WCW' in *Hwaet: Twenty Years of Ledbury Poetry Festival*, ed. Mark Fisher (Bloodaxe Books, 2016).

'Translation', from 'Humanities', appeared in *Prague Post* (2011), and was read at Ewald Osers's funeral in Ivana Bozděchová's Czech translation.

'History' is Nangle Rare Books' *Bookmark Poems* no. 10 (2015).

I am grateful to David and Elizabeth Stone for having me write 'Amos'.

# Contents

DOVES

# The Sort of Thing

The BBC does not do product placement.
The bitter in the Queen Vic, for example,
has an imaginary name. There isn't
the density of brand names we grew up with.
Jokes about Tampax came with puberty;
I remember Ariel being launched,
the first pure biological detergent;
needing a razor, I once bought a Braun
because its name implied Germanic craft,
my toothpaste's either Crest or Oral B,
Gillette is rakish and American
and I remember how affording Pampers,
thick, disposable nappies, put an end
to boiling nappies in our biggest saucepan,
and how at school we'd put a dab of Vicks
below our nostrils to evict catarrh.
All these brands are now one portfolio,
Procter & Gamble holdings, whether theirs
to start with, or through merger, by what chain
of luck or circumstance, I just don't know,
though I'm certain my father would have known.
It was the sort of thing he somehow knew,
he who once took a suitcase full of laundry
off to work, leaving by the door his briefcase.

# Jardin du Luxembourg

A young man not unlike myself at his age,
a touch less inhibited,
arm round his girl: 'We know what the point
of love is but of death, no,
nobody knows', and the coloured sails
of little boats on the pool
twitch one way then another.

# Ethics

When you're talking to housemates
You barely know, TV
Wants utter revelation,
Reality TV.

The model speaking now
Describes a former spouse
Hitting and hurting her cervix
When hot and vigorous.

It seems like overshare
But him she doesn't name,
Who could be one of several.
Only herself to blame.

Whatever the famished camera
Lurking behind a shelf
Wants, you should only ever
Pass judgement on yourself.

# Joseph Brodsky, 1940–1996

An eye drinks a seascape as cranes clang
through the smog of an early morning
in the thrice-named city your teenage

years erupt out of. You are fifteen.
You walk out of school. You are next seen
in court. A servile and obtuse judge

demands who licensed your poethood.
You belong to no union. God
perhaps? Your answer finds no purchase.

You are sentenced. Internal exile.
But you survive. External exile.
Auden finds you work in a college

and you flourish in Michigan, that
cold place. Venice, Manhattan, and at
Byzantium – anywhere tonnage

harbours you find a momentary
stay. Against confusion, poetry
erects itself in search of knowledge.

Your baroque elaborate stanzas
show us a place no whit like Kansas
or New York or an exile's village:

a cold, northern, invented city
a tsar created, where a party
proved the noblest dream can turn savage.

Sentences taut with syntax, metre
that freezes time like architecture;
what is left of a man is language.

# The Value of X

*Six is a perfect number, not because God completed all
things in six days, but rather, conversely, the reason God
completed things in six days, was because that number
was perfect even if those things did not exist.*

— ST AUGUSTINE

If, said Leibniz, God
sings to himself, he will sing
algebra.

Does God see
mathematical beauty?

Did he create it?
Or are number-relations
implicit, immutable?

There will always
be a countable difference
between one thing and two.

Between the mare we passed
this afternoon, for instance,
and her with her foal,
on its long tentative legs.

It looked
like a daddy-long-legs,
alert to race off
across surfaces
it hardly touches.

But its precarious bones
would stumble, crack.

To build numbers, you need
the empty set. Nought is the empty set.
One is the set containing the empty set.
Two is the set that contains the empty set
and the set containing the empty set.

Descartes thought we could only
be truly sure of maths.
The foal
might be a trick of God's
or a trick of the light.

It knows it isn't,
gazing toward the trees
it is discovering.

As for the numbers,
we began with counting
and went on to measure the earth,
the cosmos.

There are the stars, their distances
all known.

They look like joints
of a climbing frame
for man to inch up
when he must leave this planet.

When Eden burns
and algebra holds true.

# Il libro dei libri

Here's an omnium gatherum for you:
two myths about origins, the bitter bread of exile,
schedules of law, some ropy chronicles,
a song of loneliness, more chronicles,
some moral uplift, a shout against the cosmos,
some folklore, an atheist manifesto,
songs of protest, songs of acceptance, a sexy piece,
   a stream
of denunciation of how folk lived,
four biographies that require collation, some letters
and a dream-vision.

Some of their authors
were all-out writers,
some of them, newly literate,
shuddered in the grip of gift.

They must be read
as one deciphers potsherds.

You may
hear thunder echoing and see
strange lights along the ragged hills.

# On Reading an Obituary of
# Sir Lattimore Brown, Soul Musician

He comes home from Vietnam to find wife
A with child by another man
so takes his music on the road.

After a time he has a club.
He calls it The Atmosphere Lounge.
He takes the house band on the chitlin' circuit.

He signs with Otis Redding's agency.
Redding dies in a plane crash.
'Otis Is Gone' is his one big hit.

Wife B. Club two. B dies
after heart surgery.
No club. Wife C

dies of lung cancer
so he totes his music back on the road.
Somebody takes to using as a stage name

one too like his
and the Mafia, pissed at the mix-ups,
put out a contract on him. Fall guy,

so no more road. A third club.
Bill Clinton blows some sax there.
The club fails, time has passed, he trudges

back to the road again,
though a business bible says he's been dead
for twenty years. And then a hurricane,

Katrina, leaves him badly injured
and homeless, all his worldly goods destroyed.
Wife D (we haven't met her yet)

dies of a heart attack.
He's living in a trailer park.
He doesn't hear for five months.

He's stabbed and robbed and left for dead.
A good nurse introduces him
to a man who gets him

singing again.
He buys a new house
and is run over nearby. Killed.

That's the story of Sir Lattimore Brown
who never knew his parents.
'Sir' was his own addition

(not,
we might note, King,
Count, Duke or Earl).

Towards the end, he said
'God has blessed me.
The greatest thing in life is to let

your heart be kind
and respect others
as you would have them to do unto you.'

Hard not to laugh
at such unmitigated bad luck;
harder still not to flinch

at such nobility.
And The Atmosphere Lounge?
Failed, when the sleeping partner

went out and killed Lee Harvey Oswald.

## South Seas

A blond dream for Cavafy,
your long cool smooth
circumcised body.

You were last heard of
in the Pacific, but that
was decades back.

You were a hedonist
I suppose, certainly
a sexual one.

You adored David Bowie,
who was so openly, I see now,
what we aspired to,

measureless possibility.
Boys and girls both
desired him.

Someone had met him
and he sang 'Rock 'n' Roll Suicide'
with the someone's friend's acoustic.

A flat in London. What
we were. I envy
the long sleep of your life,

if sleep it is,
for it's a tough discipline
to be bothered

only by small things,
a torn blue aerogram,
an encroachment of sand . . .

to live out desire.

# Round Market Square

A wild old man plays the spoons
on the plinth of a nothing sculpture.
On a new college clock, a locust

pulls minutes to its jaws.
In the market, another man
with straggling white hair thumbs through old CDs.

The first acid casualties
are in their seventies or more.
Mine was at least the second generation.

In the mirror, my face
ran like a Francis Bacon
yet I also heard notes hang in the air like pearls.

I sat on a hillside, alone
with the universe, hugging my knees.
The moon looked good, shining down through the trees.

# Tina

*crystal meth*

She makes wraiths, phantoms, of the most remarkable people.
She shows you all your friends are false friends and you spend

whole weekends awake and wasted at the kind of party
where you put a rubber sheet down before the fun starts,

naked or dressed in leather, rubber, PVC or clingfilm. Boys arrive
like 3D printing from the internet. They are new friends for you.

Do I envy your abandonment to pleasure? Possibly.
But not the ashen afterwards not knowing how you got home,

not the swinging door and the money missing,
not waking scratching as though trying to tear your face off.

She speeds your speech until it is unintelligible.
Quite soon, there will only be her to talk to.

# Nocturne

I've thought of you from time to time, four decades
since you went back to your vast continent
and disappeared from small talk. Curious,
I search the Net for you. Some unrevealing
death notices and one police report.
I didn't even know that you had died.

I find your last address on Google Streetview.
It is one of two buildings, one set back.
Neither's a flophouse but they don't look much.
They've not been cared for as their neighbours have.
Your apartment's number suggests the ground floor.
At our age, when we have to start to answer
to ourselves for what we have made of life,
there should be more to show at where you lived,
bohemian and bookish, than this peeling
white paint, these cheap cars on the forecourt, surely.
I wonder whether it's some kind of shelter.
They say you were a freelance writer. Nothing
confirms this on the Net, so did you die
committed to a writing no one wanted?
Hold hopes too long that, failing, broke the spirit?
It might just be you took your own life.

Forgive me that I cannot let you go
altogether forgotten to your grave,
if that was what you wanted in the last hours.
The ignobility of your arrest,
little more than a week before you died,
makes you someone I just don't recognise,
puts you somewhere I flinch from thinking of,
drunk by mid-morning, or, your mind destroyed,
gone, flashing and swearing at a woman
from next door, someone you may have known,
who called the cops. That's on record. Their brief
report, all facts, no story, makes me want
only to think of you when we were young –

the morning, say, when somebody had heard
you weren't sure if the Grateful Dead were playing
pre- or post-revolutionary music
but you were working on it. I forget
the answer but expectancy comes back
and I recall our walk through fields one dawn
when the first bird chirped from the trees around,
then all, to ring us with ecstatic sound.

It is still dark in the world.
Already I am not a young man.

# Lament

*i.m. Dennis O'Driscoll (1954–2012)*

Rain that was tilting
against the slates
all morning gave up.

I didn't see when,
as I try not to see
the futile ambulance.

A standing stone
among the rock-knuckled
grass of the west,

braced by and against
any Atlantic weather,
a stone unnamed,

would stand for you.

# The Psalmist

When I look up
my soul is water, it
trembles beneath your breath
as the skin of a mountain pool
shakes below whistled cloud.

Where there is music
let each voice praise you,
clashing cymbals
unleash their roaring
whisper, the strings sing

at one with braided voices
of boys and girls, and let the harpist
bow her sweet
neck to the sweet burden
of an air plucked from air,

the trumpeter bray
what you have promised,
that you will move among us
to bind each wound,
that all things shall be made good.

# Amos

*Then answered Amos, and said to Amaziah, I was no prophet,
neither was I a prophet's son; but I was an herdman, and a
gatherer of sycomore fruit:*
*And the LORD took me as I followed the flock, and the
LORD said unto me, Go, prophesy unto my people Israel.*
*– Amos 7.14–15*

The city of bankers and the city of working men is one city
and it is damnable. What have we done to have made bankers out of men and faceless workers out of men? The winter
gardens and the summerhouse and the house built of ivory
all shall fall. The Old One who made the Pleiades and who
made Orion will send the sirocco with its insinuations of
the death of spirit and he will send the mildew that greens
the spine of the finest book and he will send the munching
caterpillar.

For a woman imprisoned in her leisure
the perfume of a dying flower sweetens
the long hours of a yellow afternoon.

Because the repressed returns. Before he lies down the cat on
the sofa turns round and round flattening remembered grass.

The bent blade of grass is for the ant a green bridge.

A breeze lifts and the yacht leans seaward and the manes of
grass are set streaming.

The open sea is like a hand spreading its fingers and its fingers
are open roads where all roads lead away from Rome.

It is man's nature to be lost in thought.

Acres of golden corn wait to be harvested before the rains come. The man with the sickle measures himself against those acres.

Work sings in the arm of the happy man and chokes the blood of the unhappy man.

Along the blade of grass tinier things than ants crawl with their purposes and their fleetingness. The whole earth is alive. This too is of the Old One's making.

Though its generations are dust when compared with a generation of men grass drives a patient way through concrete. Turn to the grass and be lost in the wide thought that nothing human can last but man lasts. This is both memory and promise.

# California Dreaming

Almonds and vines and lawns
knock back the shallow short-term water
then still more from the black depths
with a pull mightier than the moon's
and suck and suck. In sudden places, earth

puckers and caves. Far westward, China smokes.
Nobody notices the rains are stopping
until they have. Tableland mesas crack
and in the mountains the snowpack thins.
Meltwater dwindles to reluctant drops.

Cities gasp in the sun's unweeping stare.
Faucets cough. Families turn inward.
There must be somebody to blame.
Better ourselves than nobody.
We brag about the damage we have done

but whether we could truly dry the rain
or bake the whole earth science cannot say;
the wastefulness is ours for sure, but this fetid
heat could be a quite impersonal and planetary
adjustment, like an ice age. It might be wise

always to keep face paint and ash about us,
for when the clouds in their definitive procession
trundle off like a wagon-train, loincloth and invocation
will be the last best hope of the last woman
and last man when they find out she is pregnant.

# The West

Where the sun goes to die
some of the waking people
have work to go to.
Others have school, doctors' appointments
or nothing, but the last
are not thought to rise early.
No one knows much about them.

Drays have been and gone,
clank of barrels,
whiffs of flirtation. Cars purr.
Shadows grow sharper,
alarms are turned off,
awnings extended,
grilles folded, rattling.

The one who fears the future
cannot read the ideograms
on goods containers.
The first people,
the cleaners, the janitors,
are already free to go shopping,
as are the very old.

Papers and politicians
quarrel over the blame
for the war of a hundred years ago,
the cricket has been disappointing,
the first cuckoo has not yet hatched.
Nothing is quite in season.
On crowded trains, people fear people

who may have made
the pilgrimage to terror.
The first crosswords have been completed.
In boarding houses
there is the sound of laundry.
The man who smells of whisky
photocopies a poem for his class.

He's running late.
The future presses on his pupils.
The roses have their first buds.
Photographs of a foreign air force
landing strip among mountains
say that if justice is not shown
another justice will be.

Street-corner preachers
start their denunciations.
An archbishop goes for a jog.
A humanist is passed
to the flames in a floral coffin.
Unfashionable
policemen meet informers.

The man on a bridge
with time to spare
watches the ripples insects make.
The man who sees things
cannot say what he sees.
The man who looks at girls
looks at girls.

Primary schools have playtime.
Free voices
rise like coloured balloons.
A passer-by who paused
might feel the heavy world
lighten, her shoulders loosen,
her mind be combed, a moment.

Wind flicks her coat.
A goods train rattles.
Mid-morning
already, and the sun rises
westward and ever westward
while the worlds people make
shake as they make them.

# Humanities

I LINES WRITTEN ON THE RETIREMENT
OF MR PETER CONRAD

Passers-by in St Aldate's
spot a vanished light:
the insomniac
don has gone, in whose
hands books were old friends
with new secrets each meeting.

Tutorials were swift hours
followed by two more
– coffee, texts open –
making sense phrase by
phrase of what he'd said
until the texts themselves spoke.

The manner was a sidelong
Australian drawl,
much imitated,
and as for the shades
and black leather, I'd
swear to both. And the stuffed owl.

I've just read an elegy
for an Oxford don
by an Oxford don
in which what is praised
are the size of his
penis and his idleness:

knowing nothing of the one,
absent the other,
all we gather to
praise is the good job
greatly done by this
model unsleeping reader.


II CHALDEAN

*The Nymphs of the Fountains, and all the Water Spirits,*
*and terrestrial, aërial and astral forms, are the Lunar*
*Riders and Rulers of all Matter, the Celestial, the Starry,*
*and that which lieth in the Abysses.*
— LYDUS, *De Mensibus*

Dark matter lies
in the abysses and obeys,
as matter, law.
As yet, we do not know what law.

This dark matter is not the Chaos
the Spirit moved across.
That was the Father's
first thought,

the Father being
a fountain, pouring forth
ideas made real
through Hecate, Queen of Night.

She
sends dreams
and divinations,
owl wisdom, creeping terror.

He sends the light
that shines on all things.
How wonderful He is,
how blest

the Rulers of the Moon,
unageing girls
presiding over all
that changes.

*Thoughts of an afternoon,*
*fed by texts whose originals*
*Pico della Mirandola told*
*Marsilio Ficino*

*he owned.*
*So much to read,*
*so much to learn*
*before the night falls.*

III AUTHORITY

Dr Johnson pshawed his own achievements.
Now Scaliger, he said, he was a learned man.

Julius Caesar Scaliger, the father, botanist, critic,
    grammarian,
Aristotelian, philosopher, his learning called
    unequalled in his age,

or Joseph Justus Scaliger, the son, editor, textual
    restorer,
polyglot historian of the whole ancient world?

I have forgotten, but at seventeen I was aghast to think
    how much
must be lost at the death of any learned person.

No one can publish everything. Johnson, reporter,
    lexicographer,
tragedian, novelist, poet, essayist and critic, author

of other men's lectures, who didn't bother to read a friend's
    book
before introducing it, as he knew what it should contain,

was terrified by the parable of the talents.
One day after lunch on Salisbury Plain a colonel of artillery

said Johnson knew enough ballistics to have made
a first-rate officer. Boswell allowed that anecdote

to languish among his notes. No one can publish everything.
Long grown up, I would meet librarians who threw the old
    stock into skips

with any book not borrowed more than once a decade,
and artists who cut books up for contemporary art.

Johnson and both the Scaligers seemed as far away as
bells in abandoned towers in the wind, the sweeping wind

that was a new age howling at the too much there already,
a hateful, spiteful, levelling forgetfulness.

I am familiar with the parable.

IV TRANSLATION

*i.m. Ewald Osers (1917–2011)*

You trained as a chemist
in life.
In language
you were an alchemist.

One language melted
into another
as the translator
effaced himself,

a root from the past
pushing into the future,
nudging aside
the soil of clutter.

You kept friendships
for life,
spoke of one
that had lasted more than eighty years.

'Just a girl,' you said, 'I say a girl,
but I remember
her seventh birthday party
in Prague.'

Prague was your lost,
your golden city.
You brought the world to her.
You brought her to the world.

Jacket gone, but a sturdy
dark maroon hardback, 1951:
*The Lost Library*, by Walter Mehring.

He talks about his father's books,
how he had them fetched from Paris to Vienna
and lived with them for a year, in the Nazi time.

It is an elegy for a curriculum.
It is an elegy for humanism.
It is an elegy for Europe.

There is one impersonal neat
sharp pencil emendation
supplying an omission from some lines of Horace.

Let the schoolmaster and the pedant rejoice
with me. Like a hermit crab moving house,
something of the European mind he

believed dead had survived to read him
after the darkness and the flame, a back
stiffened to carry Horace from the rubble.

# Humboldt's Parrot

*for George Steiner*

Jangala: Sanskrit for an arid place.
Hindi cut it down to jangal. Jungle.
Alexander von Humboldt explored the jungles
of Latin America for botany, geology
and languages. Once, he came on a village
or clearing with a few huts. Loincloths, painted faces,
and a parrot making sounds that weren't pure parrot.
What were they? The language of the village
beyond the next rise, only spoken there. 'Bad neighbours,

so we killed them all, infants included, and torched their huts.'
Humboldt's heart staggers in the void surrounding it.
The bird looks at him. He looks at the bird.
Names for the cooking pot. The village saga.
Loan-words, if any. Kinship terms. Words for time and space.
He imagines the bird set free to trail the syllables
of all who died and all who died before them
across the clearing, up the next rise, flapping, squawking
over grass-matted ash and voyaging on toward the measureless.

Thirty-seven years since it left this planet, Voyager 1
leaves our solar system for a wilderness of sudden
electric gales, some forty thousand years
from its next star. It has a plaque to show
what man and woman look like, what a hydrogen atom,
where in relation to its sun it came from, pictures, recordings,
spoken greetings in many languages.
Hello from the Sumerians!
The Wu-speaking Chinese say Hi!

# 1988

In the last full year of the second Reagan
administration, all seemed setting fair
for freedom. Noble dreams were coming true.

Zeks were trekking homeward from the camps
in their first fours and fives to find what faces
waited in villages now parts of cities.

From Petersburg to Vladivostok, troubled
small people were enjoying making trouble
for the brute, the berk and the bureaucrat.

They would soon learn about insurance scams,
the speed with which poems give way to porn,
the greed that keeps the market cycle turning,

but this was spring in Europe, cleaning house
with windows open to the songs of birds.
I'm grateful to have lived at such a time

and sorry truth exacts that I add this:
eighty-eight was also the last full year
of the red threat that kept our bankers honest.

# Shingle

Once these were one
rock and of one
mind, to withstand,
so broke
into breakable pieces.

They bide
their own time,
rub up against
each other, scrape
along.

Seas have tumbled them
and fallen back.
They shoulder tide
and tempest, broken yet
of one mind.

# Come Wind

He turns up in poems, more and more poems,
that chap with sandwich-boards denouncing
protein and all its works, as though he were
a figure for the poet. I first saw him
when I was fourteen/fifteen, but already
I'd read about him somewhere as a London
fixture and feature. Now, he's read about
more than anyone ever read his message
in his childlike, frowning, obsessive script.
He was particularly hot on beans,
which he wanted us all to give up eating,
as their consumption is a cause of social
breakdown through widespread immorality,
notably of a sexual kind. He must
have started, I suppose, about the time
the scandals of an old establishment
featured call girls and Soviet attachés.
I remember a sorry little man
in a shopkeeper's brown coat, but I'm not sure.
I don't one moment think he wasn't mad
but his firmness of purpose, his unyielding
presence, come wind, come winter, come the decades,
stick, like the wild autistic sandwich-boards
he must now carry for eternity
down Oxford Street or Tottenham Court Road.

# Rome

When I hear of Detroit
that the cops consider buying a tank
to enter its dark no-go places,

that whole suburbs may be razed and put to grass,
strange pastoral
of tower-islands in a sea of plenty,

it merges with the Anglo-Saxon 'Ruin'.
Wonderful was the work     weltered by fate:
sidewalks are smashed     that withstood giants

roofs have ruptured     among ruins of towers.
The gate is gone     that was grey with frost.
Slates have been swept     aside and shattered

skewed from their service     by scything age
and the builders are buried     their businesses bust
a hundred harvestings     of humans back.

Waste finds a way     through wealth and wonder.
Lonely the lordless liegeman who wrote it
will have been, I imagine, imagining him

as my generic Anglo-Saxon poet,
seafarer, wanderer, caster of kennings:
whale-road and wilderness welcome his muse.

If we have no abiding city
but seek a city that is yet to come,
hearken to him     handhold the heathen

mourner of men     when May flowers brightest
landscape is loveliest     listen and hold.
What you inherit     the homeless unhappy

voice of veterans     vanquished by weariness
stiffens with spring     new sap in its veins
with sangfroid perceiving     in cities that die

in civilisation     sacked and besmirched
purposes poems     pungent with wreckage
moulding and mastering     mourning resume

of which cities are signs     but signs is all.

# Duende

*i.m. Robin Totton (1928–2010)*

So vehemently godless
I almost wish you non-existence . . .
In your École Normale days
a black GI said that white boy could play the blues

so small wonder so many of your last years
were given over to flamenco.
Through seven years, a six-month project
became a book with self-performed CD.

Duende in a teacher
falls hopelessly behind with marking,
fills up then scrubs the board –
'No, that's Catalan, not Italian,

forget it.' Sometimes you left the room.
I know now it was when you felt
petit mal creeping on.
The school-mag obituary

stresses your courtesy,
the quality I noticed
only the last time,
the first for years. Before, I hadn't,
which means it was the highest kind.
We swam in it like fish in a bowl,
who don't pay water much mind.

There is a photograph with friends
on Facebook.
I don't know where your grave is.

# WCW

Saxifrage, said William Carlos Williams, was his flower
because it split stone. Yesterday, in a pot, a clump of it,
weedy red petals, stems robust as peasant legs.

It would survive a summer's rage for decking,
frost memory, meltwater gush, black August.
It wouldn't last a weekend in the jungle,

being a flower of the far north, temperate at best.
Williams was a doctor, and he could listen to his language
for the slightest sign, like a stethoscope.

Saxum is stone, frag the root of frangere, to break.
Latin names for northern things. Ghosts of empire.
Williams had time for the patient ones, men, women, children

who hang on, who pull through, saxifrage splitting stone.

# Christmas Eve

It was late, and the woman pale with fear,
The husband elderly, the donkey zonked.
I wished them well, but couldn't have them here.
Travelling reps and local girls vin blanc'd
Half senseless were at full pitch in both bars,
Food flying from the kitchen and the rooms
All spoken for – not quite *Harper's Bazaar*'s
Notion of glitz, but not just ee-bah-gooms.

These rather sweet, provincial, pious folk
Wouldn't fit in and might put people off.
Horses for courses. Nods. We hardly spoke.
They left. They're born survivors. Caesar's tough
Taxes have nearly brought me to my knees.
Why should I have to harbour refugees?

# Carol

The power to annihilate
Our public and our private fate
    Is sleeping in a manger.
Be you sage or shepherd, stranger,

Lean close, then leave before he wakes
And his clear gaze clear judgment makes
    On all your works and days,
The little terror, born to raise

The dead and, yes, the living dead,
The bled by bankers, the unfed,
    And every mortal soul
That labours for its daily dole

Of pittance from the pitiless
Unceasing rasp of dailiness,
    That shivers like a child
When the nocturnal wind goes wild

About the outhouse and the things
Left out to dry. An angel sings
    And all of us are hushed
By something that will not be rushed,

The sweetness pure as heather honey,
The fortune never told in money,
    This little scrap will bring.
Yes, we have heard an angel sing

And, singing, say we've seen enough
To carry this good news through rough
   Terrain to careworn days,
New angels, with unending praise.

# Discretion

*i.m. Wisława Szymborska (1923–2012)*

Children already
learn and recite your lines,
too young to believe you
were a real person, one of them, once.

When you die, there's a small stir
in the books pages here
like the splash
in hidden water

when some tiny, shy creature
has slipped away.
A phalanx of spears,
reeds keep us off.

# Femikrimi

Mist in the trees.
An orchard. Moon.
A corpse.

The woman with gripes and hassles
like everyone comes.
She sees everything

dimly, at first. Her gift
is like a dowser's,
uncertain, fragile, sudden.

She squats, look, thinks,
her sexiness enhanced
by her not knowing that she has it.

The puzzle
is an octopus on the city,
tentacles everywhere,

old-money dining rooms,
yards with scrap metal and syringes,
the dawn quay, seagulls foghorns.

She travels light.
Finds truth
in the hour between dog and wolf.

# The Return

It is all there the same when I go back.
The woods still block the far edge of the field
but they've been thinned, their scrub severely hacked.

No crackle now of dry leaf underfoot,
unlike the night we dug the badger-trap
and covered it with twigs and leaves and dirt.

The tall headmaster summoned me next lunchtime.
The groundsman had been out to shoot some pigeons
and fallen in. His gun fired as he fell.

He could have died. I must apologise
in person, so I did, the only words
I said at that time to that scowling man.

But later, when I taught there for a term,
I got to know him, just a little. One
morning, he told me he collected birdsong

and took me to his shed, where he hung up
his bleak tan mac and, from a shelf of tapes,
played me a range of trills and cheeps and squawks

as his tight, wrinkled, weather-darkened face
turned bright and childlike, purity of joy
and wild delight possessing him completely.

I know the tall headmaster and at least
two of my friends are in their graves. And he?
It was clear there was no point even asking.

Half the staff had been born since I went back
the first time, none of them was working there.
When I brought up the ancient wooden playhouse

and the rat we saw running under it,
they said it was pulled down twelve years ago.
As they recalled the changing rooms and office,

it came to me the building they described
had occupied the space where mine had been;
British Bulldog on rainy afternoons,

the bars for climbing, the hot hairy ropes,
that sweet well-water from a rusty tap,
were immemorially long ago

for them, and further for the jerseyed children,
who asked good questions when I read my poems
in the library, once a kitchen garden.

I felt no feeling when I felt for one.
The past had been so utterly erased,
the last bird of a species being shot . . .

I have forgotten where we found the spade.
I didn't meet my ghost, so I suppose
he left and grew up and is my age now,

or the ghost of the badger that never was,
carried in triumph in a laundry basket,
the unforgettable raw stink of it.

# Heaven's Gate

*for Joanne*

You lead me through a dark wood. We come out
onto a grass stage, and the view explodes:

however wide you flung your arms, you couldn't
start to embrace those cubic miles of air

or the reasoned eighteenth-century spread
below, great house and grounds, white picturesquely

self-dotting sheep, a lake, an island. Sky
is drawn into the gardener's harmony.

This is the good place, it attests; look down
at this as you would at the Promised Land.

# Doves

*i.m. Seamus Heaney (1939–2013)*

I

Two collared doves came and sat
on my open window all spring. She
had a damaged feather and the more trusting nature.
She would lay her head on his breast
and watch me. Daily, they came and went, fetching
a litter of twigs they dropped on the windowsill.
They were like raw newly-weds
knowing they should make a home, not yet knowing
    how.
One morning,
there was an egg on top of the window.
It lasted two days.

After a few weeks, neither of them
flew away when I pulled the curtains open.
I talked to them.
I thought about St Francis.
I thought about love
as they revealed it.

Then he grew cocksure and squeezed
into the room as I'd thought he couldn't.
Crossed a line I hadn't considered.
The mess and broken plants were too much.
I pulled the window closer.
It left too little room for them.
They never came again
and I felt I had violated all their trust.

They weren't symbolic or a message
but simply what they were, a visitation,
not of ghosts, not of memories, but of something
unstained and pure.


II


'Thole'.
That was the word you focused on,
thinking of things we say when someone dies.
Along with 'He'll be missed'
you remembered 'You'll have to thole'.

Endure. Suffer.
Be patient, in the sense of undergoing,
without complaint, great pain.

As the Spartan boy hugged the fox
that feasted on his guts.

Self-discipline
will keep us civil.


III


I remember you lit up
at an Irish Embassy party.
You had been kind to Wendy and to me.
That was the night you held us both
in one big hug.
Then you read and the room was clapping.

IV

You weren't hurt into poetry
but lured to it,
trout to the fly,
by the relish of sounds
that rang truest
when informed by the home, or,
increasingly, by Latin.

Poeta doctus, surely.

It was the country boy's
gape and gawp at the world, though,
through which so much
came in to be transfigured.

And bewilderment at the wilderness men make
of what is human or humane.

And understanding why.

V

Two collared doves came and sat
on my open window all spring,

birds, yet a visitation
of something pure, unstained.

Visitations and intimations,
bread for the spirit to be found

everywhere daily,
would we only allow ourselves

to marvel. Poetry's task
is the marvellous in the ordinary

and losses to be tholed.

# Afternoons

*for SC*

Between us now there is nothing.
A damp beach under massed cloud.
No rain. Darkness where the cloud meets the sea.

I miss our afternoons of tea and talk,
your Iris Murdochs, long skirts and glasses.

Some fool told you I was in love with you.
I wasn't. I was too gauche to say so
in our terse interview. Friendship roadkill.

Between us now there is nothing.
A damp beach under still cloud.
Unbroken procession of unbreaking waves.

They shift some bits of tethered weed
back and forth like a masked dementia.

# Meinong's Jungle

Existence,
Alexius Meinong said,
is just a property an object
may or may not possess.

Mountains possess it
but not the golden mountain,
the wooden iron.

Objects that don't possess it
are of two kinds,
impossible and possible.

A winged horse is impossible,
what an unanswered prayer sought
might yet be given,

so they are neighbours
in a kind of jungle or junkyard
where anything that can be
without existing finds
its mode of being.

The Tory conscience.
The Liberal spine.
The Labour ethic.

The perfect poems.

Sometimes the veil
is lifted and the odd
black swan escapes.

# Will's Brothers

### I GILBERT (1566–1612)

I was a haberdasher.
I made a bob or two in London
and then I went home,
liking a more
companionable river.

Buttons, ribbons and furbelows
and things for men.
I gave Will special terms.
He paid at once.
Debt terrified him.

As a child, I was appalled
when Edmund turned up.
Who likes to imagine
their parents doing that?
I sulked all afternoon.

I suppose I looked after Richard.
I once stood bail
for another Stratford man,
William Sampson,
maker of clocks.

Sampson's clocks were only clockish,
Will pronounced as a youth,
which made him Samson Stockfish.
He later used it in a play.
He was impossible.

Childhood never quite worked for me.
Sister Joan was a bit dry.
Married a hatter. Says it all.
But Will, I ask you. If it wasn't
one thing it was another

would set him chortling,
red-faced, spitting bread.
Gag after gag,
like somebody afraid of silence.
Hit or miss, funny or no.

When Hamnet died,
he said he couldn't stake his
heart on another son.
He brought Edmund up but he never
treated this brother like his own son

though Edmund was his image,
vital, funny.
No wonder
he turned out as he did,
Will in most ways

but in a borrowed costume,
hoping he might
one day impress
his father-brother.
I kept away from all that,

followed my own path.
I made no marriage.
I walked beside the river
where I was loved once
and where I loved.

The golden lads
all came to dust.
If I could, as I did,
survive the plague,
it was to be a kindly uncle.


II RICHARD (1574–1613)

Edmund's birth made me wonder.
By then, it might have been beyond our father
to work out whether or not this mewling little scrap was his

or not. A bastard. No one breathed it.
Nobody could have thought it of our mother.
But the old man could hardly be compared with Abraham,

wheezing complaints between sups
or, like the sun through a low mist on the river,
musing over the glory days when he was the Guild incarnate.

I saw him wheedle.
I heard my mother lying to his creditors.
These are not things a child should ever see.

Sister Joan was busy.
Sister Anne died when she was seven
and I was just five. Her funeral was our parents' last big
   fling.

I curled up and was quiet.
In the end, nobody noticed me.
All I could threaten was the new baby in the cradle

and that I did. I cursed it
with every vile word father ever uttered.
I made some up by changing nouns to verbs and so forth.

I was a dark shadow
removed as soon as he could speak and tell on me.
Not from his dreams, his troubled sleep, his thrashing.

I'd hardly known Will
before he'd gone, and when he came back
it was his wife, long private talks with our mother about
   the future,

propping the bar with old friends
or shocking Gilbert with suggestive sallies.
I was grown up before he chose to confide in me.

He said 'Being called England's Ovid
doesn't matter much when the big news
is the price of sheep and the vicar's latest innovations'

as though I'd understand that was why
he loved it all, the fairs, the fairings and the pairings,
the parish pomp, the summer bubbles in a dozing stream,

why he remembered all
the local words and family names for things
long after most who'd been away forgot all that,

why he remembered
old people's old saws, rumours
of witches, fairies, lunacies, and his teacher's mannerisms.

It was as though he'd taken
our childhood with him in a little box
and brought it back with all its colours sharpened.

I came to resent him
as fiercely as I loathed his likeness,
our pampered, pretty, poisonous benjamin

who never came back.
I stayed and made my living,
listening to the axle of the seasons grind.

I was the plodder.
I was the ant in the fable.
I didn't marry. That was my revenge.


III EDMUND (1580–1607)

Our old dad dead,
my brother took on headship of the family.
He was now thirty-seven. I was twenty-one.
He'd been married since I was two.
He'd been playing the part for years.

I grew up with the children.
Oldest, I led our games.
Susanna, Daddy's girl,
pert, sexy, scary, brilliant.
Hamnet, bright hope, too young to know
what he might promise, died.
Judith, who made us laugh and went to the bad,
married and ran a tough house. Raucous, unseemly lass,
but little then. We all were.

Distracted, gripped, he'd hold the table silent
with the gaze of his wandering inward eye.
I wondered if it helped pull women.
He would scream in his sleep if he saw
horrible things.
He'd smile and say 'I word them, that's
the trick of it.'
He'd be away for months
then lantern, horse, half-muffled face.
He loved his children's flash of recognition.
He scattered oranges and toys. He marvelled
at how they'd grown or changed. At how I had.

I followed him to London
before our father died.
Acted. Better, I like to think,
than he did. In a different theatre.
Grew a small name,
had many friends, chased women, drank
where he did not. Mistress and small boy. Edward.
Someone misspelled him Edward Sharksbye. Names
dissolve and dissipate.

I'd not go back to Stratford.
London was a release. You could be anyone.
I never knew
how he bore his unutterably dull friends
on their treadmill of births, marriages, deaths and work

and I wouldn't haunt Stratford now,
where, at theatre-time, empty restaurants lurk
like pike.

How trapped
in words he was, words
black as the veins in marble.

His Edgar, that
absolute dreary nothing, talks himself
into being a person fit for kingship
by speaking whirling madness.

I died at twenty-seven.
I imagine
my family, his family,
my sisters who were not my sisters,
nieces who called me uncle as a joke –

Susanna, look up from your book!
Judith, freeze mid-pour!

To Edgar's bastard brother,
the most engaging, hollowest,
most frivolously wicked
of all his villains, my brother gave
his brother's name.

# Crem

At the dismal
humanist funeral
they'd asked a cousin to preside,
a priest.

There was time
for reflection but not for prayer.
At the very end,
curtains

about to close around the coffin,
she leant over it, made the sign of the cross
and blessed it
furtively, like a dissident.

# Death in the Neighbourhood

The things, which cannot mourn, mourn.
Metal animals in the sun
where she sat last summer,
laughing, recovered, tanning,
have lost their purpose and stare
into the world of things,
jetsam and scrap they were saved from
by an eye that is closed.

I saw the private ambulance,
the two men in dark suits and ties,
and guessed. Today
the curtains of the room where she lay
are open, a last
flower not drooping yet.
It will not be lit tonight
or again before new people come.

The daughter lives elsewhere,
likewise the son.
There'll be no obituaries
unless it's mentioned, perhaps,
in an old pupils' newsletter
and someone looks up to say
'I sometimes wondered
what had become of her.'

Friends and family grieve
but the things will close their hearts.
They'll mean a bit
for a bit then they'll disappear,
be sold or scrapped
or just lost. Rusting.
The new people won't need to know.
We shan't be here forever.

# Home

*for* W

I

Sparks wafted up
to settle on black branches.
They winked and died
suddenly, silently,

under the night. The bonfire
got a grip on itself and roared.
Shooting sparks.
Because this was a school

leaves of chemistry, leaves of autumn, flew
into the fire. You watched it all,
cheeks, eyes, bright
answering warmth.

II

Dark miles, flickering houses and the gaunt stars.
By the time we're home, we're in frontier country.
A plant scrapes the fence. The rickety thing
holds, and the tops of trees are white with moonfire.

III

Sides of an empty lorry
go woop-woop
like a wobble-board, woop

through the milkbottle clank
of the chassis
bouncing along.

It would like to fall apart
completely,
as at my wits' end I did.

A knackered lorry.
A-woop-a-woop-a.
Clankety-clankety-clank.

IV

You held. You held me through the grey and grey
days and nights of a long depression.
You live with me and are my love, my bright
answering warmth, though leaves of autumn fly.

## Stars

We thought to bring the stars
down to earth, like we are.
We built them concrete
and metal columns
to perch on. They only gave
a stranger
lonelier light.